First Fabulous Facts

Dinosaurs

Written by Jaclyn Crupi

Illustrated by Patrizia Donaera

Cartoon illustrations by Jane Porter

Consultant: Dr Darren Naish

Educational consultant: Geraldine Taylor

A catalogue record for this book is available from the British Library

Published by Ladybird Books Ltd
80 Strand, London, WC2R 0RL
A Penguin Company

001
© LADYBIRD BOOKS LTD MMXIII
LADYBIRD and the device of a Ladybird are trademarks of Ladybird Books Ltd

ISBN: 978-0-71819-353-9

Printed in China

Contents

What were dinosaurs?

Dinosaurs were reptiles that walked the Earth for 165 million years, during a time called the Mesozoic era. They died out more than 63 million years before the first humans appeared.

Quetzalcoatlus

Alamosaurus

Plioplatecarpus

Triceratops

Fabulous Facts

Fancy feathers

Some dinosaurs, like Citipati, had feathers and a beak, but most couldn't fly.

Tough scales

Many dinosaurs, like Albertosaurus, had tough, scaly skin just like lizards have today.

Close friends

Flying pterosaurs, such as Quetzalcoatlus, and water creatures, like Plioplatecarpus, lived at the same time and were closely related to the dinosaurs.

They're amazing!

Body skills

Some dinosaurs, like Stegosaurus, had hard plates on their back to help regulate their body temperature.

Fossil finds

Fossils are the remains of dead animals and plants. Fossils found in the earth or in rocks show us what dinosaurs may have looked like, how they might have lived and what the Earth was like when they were alive.

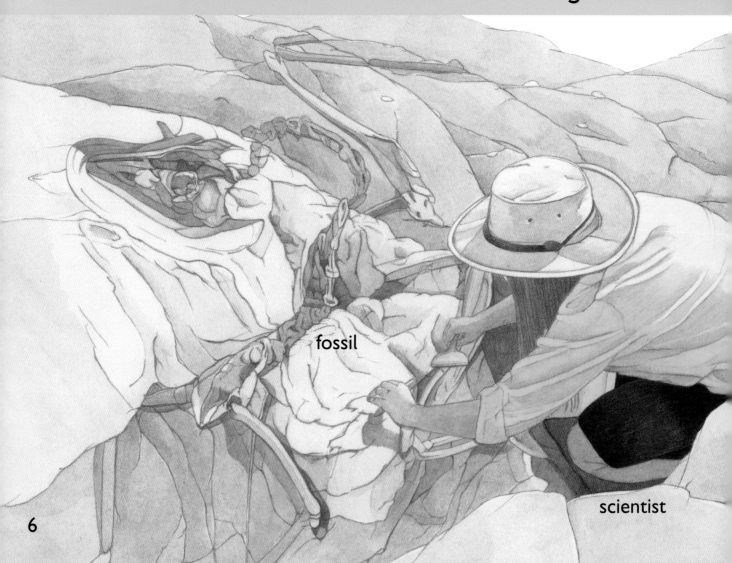

fossil

scientist

Fabulous Facts

Buried bones

When a dinosaur died, the hard parts of its body, like teeth and bones, were often buried in the mud. Over time, these turned into stone and became fossils.

Prehistoric patterns

Some fossils formed when the leaves of a fern made a pattern in the mud.

Dinosaur hide-and-seek

Skin doesn't form fossils, so nobody knows what colour dinosaurs were. Most were probably the same colours as the world around them to give them camouflage.

Can you see me?

Wow!

Scientists hunt for, and study, dinosaur fossils. They clean up fossil finds and piece them together to make a dinosaur's skeleton.

What is this?

BIGGEST dinosaurs

The largest creatures that have ever lived on Earth were plant-eating dinosaurs called sauropods, like Brachiosaurus. Sauropods had long necks for reaching high into trees, long tails, strong legs and tiny heads.

Brachiosaurus

Fabulous Facts

Biggest of them all

The biggest known sauropod was Amphicoelias. It was about 50 metres long and weighed 100 tonnes – the same as twelve elephants.

I love see-saws!

Hello up there!

Longest neck

Mamenchisaurus had a neck 13 metres long with nineteen neck bones. Most dinosaurs had only nine or ten neck bones! Mamenchisaurus would have reached as high as a four-storey house.

Wow!

Diplodocus was about 26 metres long – as long as two buses! At 14 metres, its tail was probably the longest of all the dinosaurs.

SMALLEST dinosaurs

Not all dinosaurs were huge. Some were quite small.
Many of the tiniest dinosaurs were meat-eaters.
Their small size made them fast-moving hunters.

Dinky dino

Anchiornis was a small
feathered dinosaur. It was
only 35–40 centimetres
long – smaller than
a chicken.

Hello
shorty!

Tiny terrors

These tiny dinosaurs
were only 40–50
centimetres long –
smaller than a pet
cat. They probably
ate insects, lizards
and small mammals.
Parvicursor may
have eaten termites.

Mahakala

Parvicursor

Fabulous Facts

Flying dinosaur

Unlike most dinosaurs, Archaeopteryx could fly. It was around 50 centimetres long, with sharp teeth and clawed wings.

Lightweight

Fruitadens was 65–75 centimetres long and weighed no more than 1 kilogram. That's less than a bag of sugar!

You're so sweet!

Wow!

Micropachycephalosaurus was a small dinosaur with a very long name! It was only about a metre long – just a little bit smaller than you!

I'm longer than you!

Spikes and armour

The bodies of plant-eating dinosaurs were made to protect them from predators. Many had spikes, horns, or plates made of bone. Triceratops may have used their horns when fighting each other.

Triceratops

Fabulous Facts

Protective armour

Kosmoceratops had horns above its eyes and nose, and spines on its cheeks and around its frill.

Fang-tastic

Heterodontosaurus had fangs that might have been used to bite attackers.

Super spiky

Amargasaurus had two rows of sharp spines along its neck, body and tail.

Yikes! Spikes!

Wow!

Euoplocephalus had heavy armour on its head and a bony club at the end of its tail. It even had armoured eyelids!

Super armour!

13

Mighty meat-eaters

Many meat-eating dinosaurs, like Tyrannosaurus rex, were theropods. They had strong, sharp teeth and deadly claws. Good eyesight and a powerful sense of smell helped them hunt.

Tyrannosaurus rex

Fabulous Facts

Tiny but speedy

Velociraptor was a small meat-eater, less than 2 metres tall. It had strong back legs so it could run very fast to catch its prey.

Killer claws

Deinonychus hunted large prey in packs and had clawed hands and feet that it used to attack its prey.

Snap!

Baryonyx was a fish-eating dinosaur with jaws like a crocodile.

Wow!

Daspletosaurus was a meat-eater with very long teeth — up to 18 centimetres long! That's about twice as long as your hand.

15

Hungry plant-eaters

Most dinosaurs were plant-eaters, called herbivores. Some herbivores had blunt teeth for stripping leaves and twigs from trees that they then swallowed whole. Nigersaurus had several rows of tiny teeth, which allowed it to bite tough leaves.

Nigersaurus

Fabulous Facts

Big tummies

Herbivores ate a lot so they had very big tummies. They walked on all fours as they needed the support of all four legs.

I love my food!

Tummy trouble

Sauropods ate so much that the leaves and pine needles in their tummies must have made a lot of gas!

Burp!

Tasty treats

Some plants that dinosaurs ate, including ginkgo, ferns and conifers, are still found today.

ginkgo

fern

conifer

Wow!

Hadrosaurus was a plant-eating dinosaur with a beak. It also had more than 900 teeth inside its cheeks!

Reptiles in the air

Flying animals called pterosaurs lived at the same time as the dinosaurs. Pterosaurs had furry bodies and long, pointed jaws for catching prey. They may have eaten insects, fish and even small dinosaurs.

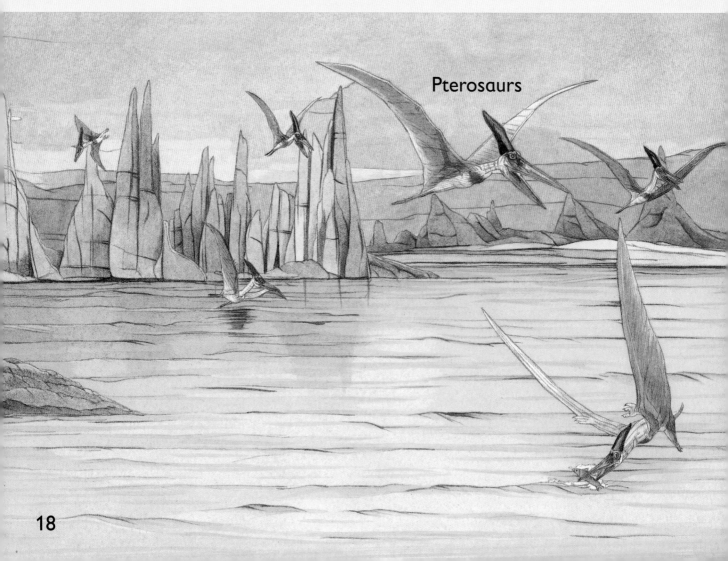

Pterosaurs

Fabulous Facts

Taking a walk

Pterosaurs had wings and could fly. On land, they probably walked on all fours, using the fingers on the ends of their wings to help them grip the ground.

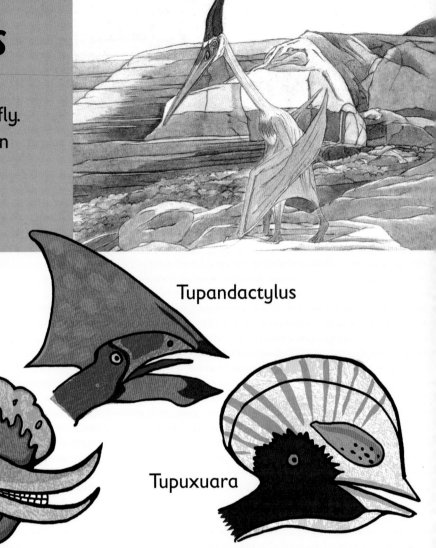

Colourful crests

Many pterosaurs had large, brightly-coloured crests on their heads. Scientists think they may have been used for display to warn off rival pterosaurs.

Tupandactylus

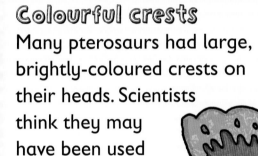

Tupuxuara

Dsungaripterus

Wow!

Some pterosaurs were the size of a small bird and others were as big as an old-fashioned fighter plane. Quetzalcoatlus was the biggest pterosaur with a wingspan of nearly 10 metres.

Race you!

Ocean hunters

There were also prehistoric water animals. Plesiosaurs had long necks and flippers to help them move through the water. They had sharp teeth for crunching fish and shellfish, such as ammonites.

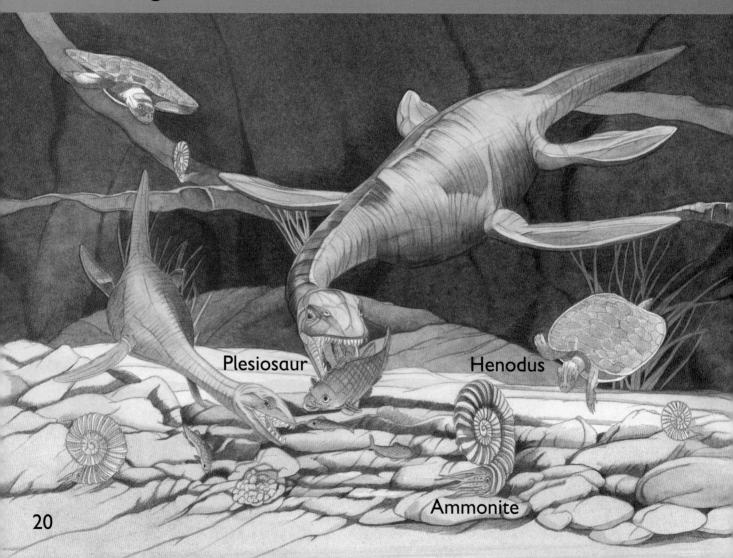

Plesiosaur

Henodus

Ammonite

Fabulous Facts

Lookalike

Ichthyosaurs looked a bit like giant dolphins with pointed fins and sharp teeth.

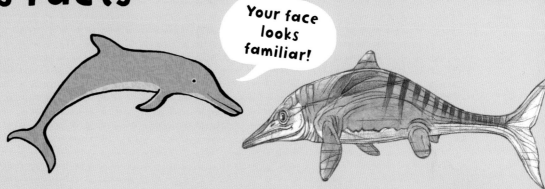

Your face looks familiar!

Crunchy lunch

Henodus looked a lot like today's turtles. It ate shellfish, which it caught with its beak-shaped mouth.

I'm feeling peckish!

Killers of the deep

Mosasaurus was 15 metres long. Its huge jaws were strong enough for it to attack other plesiosaurs.

Wow!

Elasmosaurus's neck was 7 metres long – half its entire body length!

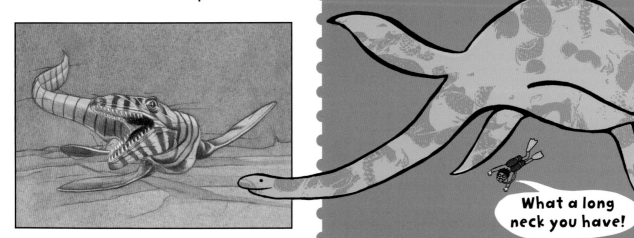

What a long neck you have!

Living together

Plant-eaters, like Centrosaurus, may have lived in groups. This would have helped protect them from predators. Most meat-eating dinosaurs lived alone.

Centrosaurus

Fabulous Facts

Pack attack

Smaller meat-eaters, like Velociraptor, hunted in groups in order to attack bigger, stronger dinosaurs.

On the road

Families of dinosaurs may have travelled together in herds to look for food.

Let's go!

Loud and proud

Parasaurolophus warned others in the herd of danger by trumpeting through its hollow crest.

Wow!

Dinosaur fossils are often found by accident. Rain and wind can wear away rock to reveal fossils beneath its surface.

I wonder where they were going...

23

Dinosaur babies

Dinosaurs laid eggs, just like reptiles and birds do today. Rather than looking after their babies, most dinosaurs laid their eggs and then left them. There were some, like Maiasaura, who looked after their babies until they were old enough to leave the nest.

nest

Maiasaura

Fabulous Facts

All shapes and sizes

Dinosaur eggs were different shapes and sizes. A sauropod egg was round like a football, while an oviraptor egg was shaped more like a potato.

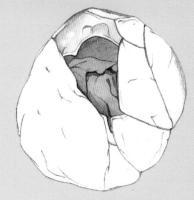

sauropod egg   oviraptor egg

Oviraptor baby

Some eggs have even been found with the fossil bones of baby dinosaurs still inside.

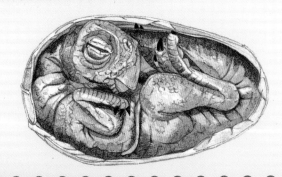

Egg pile

Some dinosaurs laid about twenty eggs. Sauropods may have laid as many as 40.

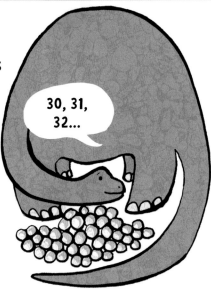

30, 31, 32...

Catch me if you can!

Wow!

Dinosaur babies grew very quickly. Many would have been able to walk or run away from danger as soon as they had hatched.

25

Where did the dinosaurs go?

Nobody really knows why the dinosaurs disappeared, but scientists are trying to find out. Some think it was because a huge meteorite hit the Earth, causing the dinosaurs to suddenly die out.

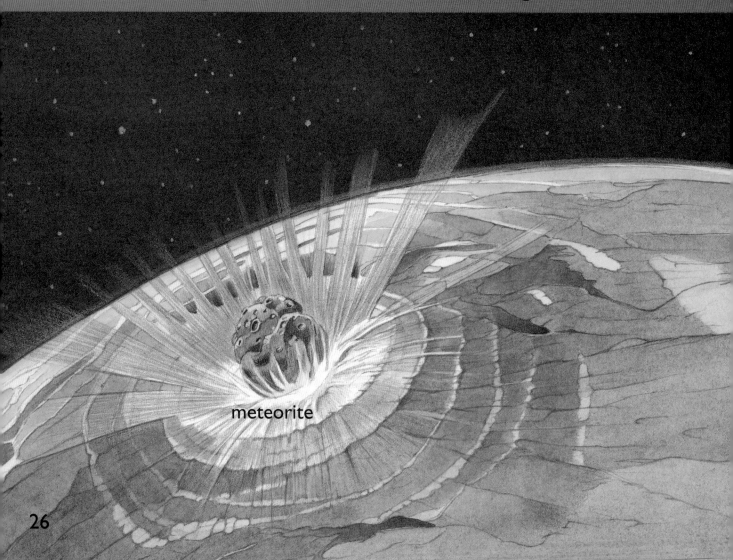

meteorite

Fabulous Facts

Super volcanoes

Another idea is that huge volcanoes erupted, sending up clouds of dust which hid the sun so the dinosaurs died of cold.

Who's a pretty birdy?

It is possible to find living relatives of the dinosaurs. Scientists have proven that the birds we see today and the dinosaurs of the past have the same sort of bones and skeletons.

My great-great-grandma was a T rex!

Wow!

Some creatures that existed during prehistoric times are still found today! The ancestors of today's crocodiles lived at the same time as the dinosaurs. Scientists are not sure why they did not die out when the dinosaurs became extinct.

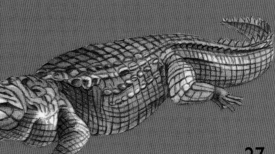

27

Record breakers

Biggest fossil

The largest fossil found so far is that of a sauropod. It is more than 30 metres long (as long as three buses). It was found in the USA.

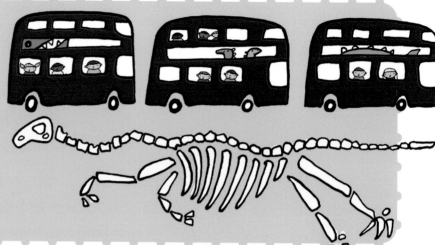

Biggest meat-eater

Spinosaurus could be up to 18 metres long, and weigh as much as 20 tonnes. Its head shape is similar to modern crocodiles. This dinosaur lived and hunted in water and on land.

Slowest walkers

With their four short legs and huge bodies, sauropods such as Seismosaurus were slow movers. They plodded at about the same speed as you and I.

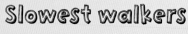

Fiercest hunter

Tyrannosaurus rex had the most powerful bite. Its jaws could be up to 1.2 metres long.

Fastest runners

The fastest dinosaurs were probably Gallimimus and Ornithomimus. They could run at about 69 kilometres per hour – that's as fast as an ostrich!

Biggest head

Pentaceratops had the largest dinosaur head. Its skull was up to 3 metres long, but it had a very small brain!

Prehistoric names

Alamosaurus	ah-la-mow-SORE-us	Maiasaura	my-ah-SORE-ah
Albertosaurus	al-BERT-uh-SORE-us	Mamenchisaurus	MAH-men-chi-SORE-us
Amargasaurus	A-MARG-uh-SORE-us	Micropachycephalosaurus	MIKE-row-pak-ee-keff-ah-loh-SORE-us
Ammonite	AM-on-ite	Mosasaurus	MOES-ah-SORE-us
Amphicoelias	Am-fi-SEEL-ee-as	Nigersaurus	NEE-zhur-SORE-us
Anchiornis	AN-kee-OR-nis	Ornithomimus	orn-ITH-oh-MIME-us
Archaeopteryx	ark-ee-OPT-er-icks	oviraptor	OHV-ih-RAP-tor
Baryonyx	bah-ree-ON-icks	Parasaurolophus	par-a-SORE-oh-LOAF-us
Brachiosaurus	BRAK-ee-uh-SORE-us	Parvicursor	PA-vih-kur-sor
Centrosaurus	cent-TROH-sore-us	Pentaceratops	PEN-tah-SERRA-tops
Citipati	chit-i-puh-tih	plesiosaur	PLEE -see-oh-SORE
Daspletosaurus	das-PLEE-toe-SORE-us	Plioplatecarpus	PLY-oh-PLAT-ee-CAR-pus
Deinonychus	die-NON-i-kus	pterosaur	TERR-uh-SORE
Diplodocus	di-PLOH-doh-kus	Quetzalcoatlus	KWET-zal-koh-AT-lus
Dsungaripterus	SUNG-ah-RIP-ter-us	sauropod	SORE-uh-pod
Elasmosaurus	eh-LAZ-mo-SORE-us	Seismosaurus	SIZE-moh-SORE-us
Euoplocephalus	you-op-loh-SEF-ah-lus	Spinosaurus	SPINE-uh-SORE-us
Fruitadens	FROO-ta-denz	Stegosaurus	STEG-uh-SORE-us
Gallimimus	gal-ee-MIME-us	theropod	THAIR-uh-pod
Hadrosaurus	HAD-row-SORE-us	Triceratops	try-SERRA-tops
Henodus	HEN-oh-dus	Tupandactylus	TOO-pan-dak-tie-lus
Heterodontosaurus	HET-er-oh-DON't-oh-sore-us	Tupuxuara	TOO-poo-HWAR-ah
Ichthyosaurs	ICK-thee-uh-SORES	Tyrannosaurus rex	tie-RAN-oh-SORE-us rex
Kosmoceratops	KOZ-moh-SERRA-tops	Velociraptor	vel-OSS-ee-rap-tor
Mahakala	mah-ha-KAH-la		

Glossary

camouflage The colour of skin or feathers which makes an animal look the same as its surroundings to hide it from predators.

crest A tuft of feathers, fur or skin on the top of an animal's head.

extinct Refers to an animal species that has died out.

fossil The remains of animals or plants that lived long, long ago.

frill A large, bony area at the back of the head of some dinosaurs.

herd A group of plant-eating animals that live and feed together.

mammal A warm-blooded animal with a hairy body and a backbone.

pack A group of meat-eating animals of the same type.

plate A thin, hard, flat shape along a dinosaur's back or body.

predator An animal that hunts another animal for food.

prehistoric Belonging to a time before history was written down.

prey An animal hunted by another animal for food.

reptile A cold-blooded animal that lays eggs.

scale A small, thin plate that protects the skin of reptiles or fish.

Index

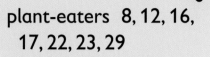